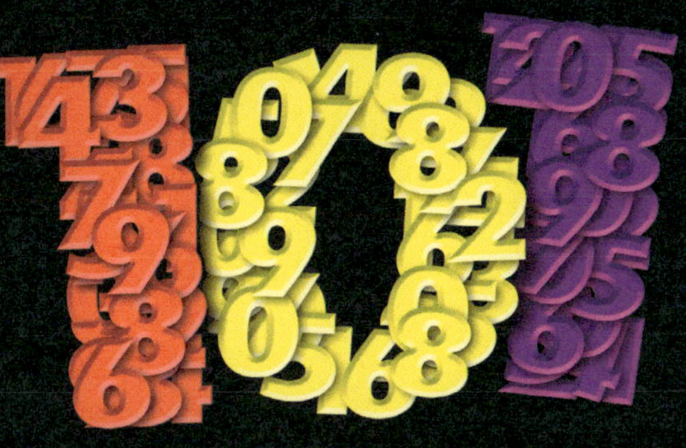

Ways to Save Earth Before Bedtime

Paul Mason

CONTENTS

1 SENDING OUT AN SOS

Earth is an amazing place. It is full of special environments – mountains, oceans, deserts and rainforests, to name just a few. Earth is also home to millions of plant and animal species. But Earth is in danger. Why? Well, because of us. Humans are doing things that are bad for the planet.

What's the problem?

Global warming is what we call the rise in Earth's temperature. That might *sound* like a good thing, but even the smallest rise in temperature can have *big* effects on the planet.

Global warming brings about:

- rising sea levels, which are bad for coastal areas
- changes in our weather, such as more extreme storms
- a decrease in our food supply because some of the world's farmland is becoming too dry to grow things.

How global warming happens

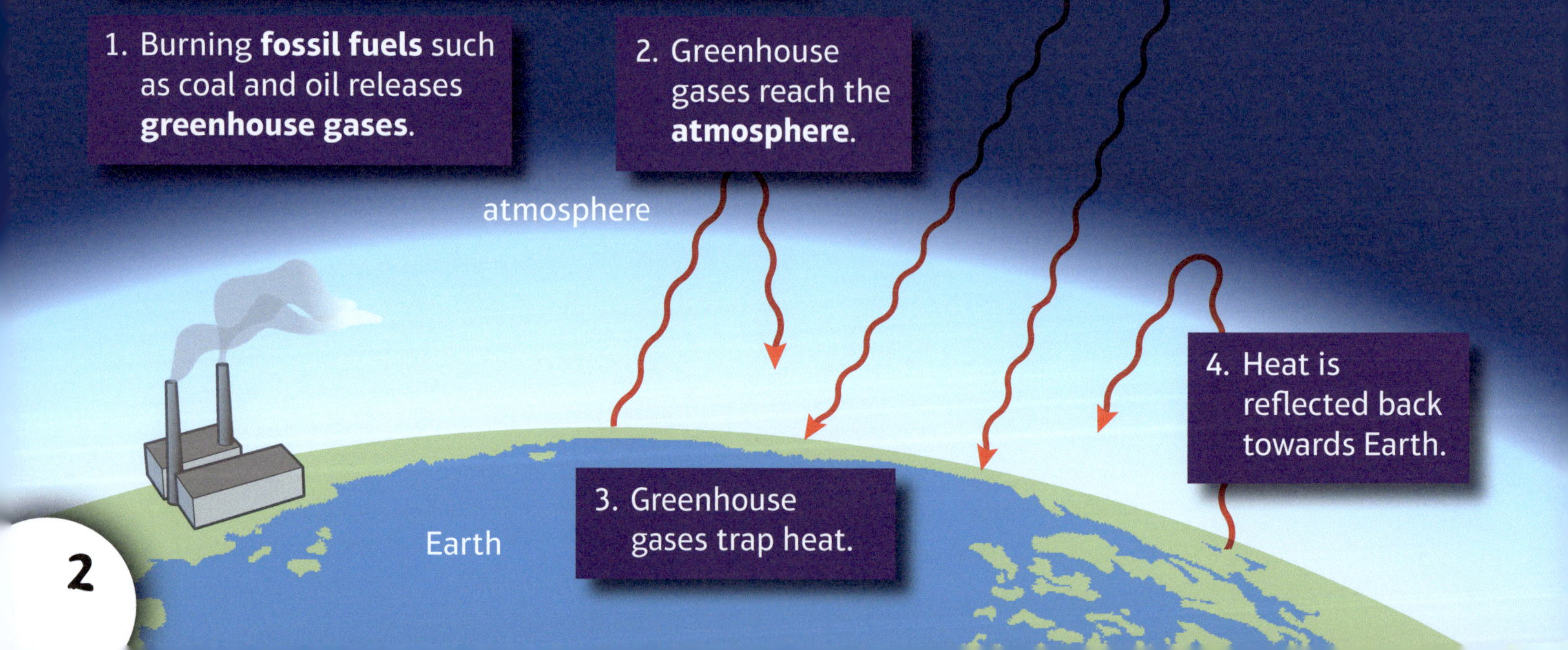

1. Burning **fossil fuels** such as coal and oil releases **greenhouse gases**.
2. Greenhouse gases reach the **atmosphere**.
3. Greenhouse gases trap heat.
4. Heat is reflected back towards Earth.

Sun

atmosphere

Earth

Can we save the world?

Earth has a lot of resources such as water, food, wood and fossil fuels. However, we are using them up too quickly and they will not last forever.

Sounds scary, doesn't it? But don't worry! You can help to save Earth – one small step at a time. Here are 101 ways how …

1 **Start Now!**

Try one idea from this book before you go to bed today. Easy!

Top Tip!

This book is special – you can start reading wherever you want! So, why not start in the middle?

WATCH OUT FOR FLYING FOOD!

Did you know that you can help save Earth by not eating flying food?

What on Earth does this mean?

At certain times of the year, some foods do not grow in Australia but will be growing in other places around the world. So these foods are flown into Australia to be sold. This is *bad* because:

- they travel a long way on aeroplanes, which burns lots of fossil fuels
- aeroplanes release greenhouse gases high up in the atmosphere where they do the most harm!

Tomatoes do not grow well in Australia in winter and spring, but they grow very well in summer. So, this summer, why not grow some tomatoes of your own?

FAST FACT
Food from far away is often grown in poor countries and bought cheaply.

1. Collect seeds from a tomato and dry them.

2. Put soil in a clean yoghurt tub. Make a hole, drop in a seed, and cover with soil.

Top Tip!
Seeds collected from a tomato grown in Australia will grow better here than those from a tomato from another country.

12 **Keep Checking**
Make sure you check that your worms have enough food waste to eat!

13 **Crack an Egg**
Sprinkle egg shells around your plants to stop snails eating them.

14 **Gumboot Pots**
Use your old gumboots as plant pots. Put some holes in the sides to stop plants becoming waterlogged.

15 **Scare the Birds**
Hang old CDs from some string over your vegetable patch to scare the birds away.

16 **Water Without Waste**
Use a watering can rather than a hose. It uses less water.

17 **Clean Your Plate**
Only fill your plate with what you can eat, and then there won't be any waste.

18 **Recycle a Christmas Tree**
Recycle your Christmas tree – a real tree, that is, not a plastic one! Some get chipped. Others are left whole and used to make sand dunes more stable!

Top Tip!
Don't give your worms too much food waste at once – feed them slowly!

19 EAT LESS COW!

Want to know one of the biggest causes of global warming? Cows! Cows fart and burp out methane, which is a greenhouse gas.

Why are there so many cows?

Well, because a lot of people eat beef. If we all ate less beef, there would be fewer cows and less cow methane!

Take the veggie burger challenge!

You will need:

1 grown-up
oil
4 cups of chopped mushrooms
1/2 cup of chopped onion
1/3 cup of grated cheese
3/4 cup of breadcrumbs
2/3 cup of oats
2 beaten eggs
salt and pepper

FAST FACT

Methane is 25 times worse for the planet than carbon dioxide, which is the greenhouse gas released by burning fossil fuels.

- First, find a grown-up to help you.
- Heat a little oil in a pan.
- Fry the mushrooms and onions for about 10 minutes.
- Mix everything together in a bowl.
- Leave for 15 minutes.
- Roll the mixture into balls and press flat.
- Put the burgers in the oven to cook.
- Put in a roll and eat!

20 Choose Chicken

Chickens have a smaller effect on the environment than cows. Make sure you choose **free-range** chicken.

21 Learn to Love Tofu

Tofu is meat-free but has lots of the same **nutritional** goodness as meat.

22 Make Your Parents Happy

Eat more vegetables!

23 Go Veggie

Be a vegetarian for the day.

24 Relax!

Are you a vegetarian? Then your work here is done.

25 Learn a Recipe

OK, when I said your work was done, I was kidding. Teach a friend how to make your favourite vegetarian meal.

26 Leave Out the Leather

Try to wear less leather because most leather comes from cows.

27 MAKE FRIENDS WITH A SPIDER

We don't mean invite your new spider friend to a movie, we just mean you should be nice to them – they're important!

How can spiders help save the world?

There's nothing a spider likes more than eating lots of tasty insects. So the next time you see a spider's web, be friendly and leave it alone.

Spiders are an important part of the **food chain**. The food chain keeps things in balance. Without spiders, there would be too many insects in the world. Also, small birds love to eat tasty spiders, but they would go hungry if spiders disappeared. The food chain works like this:

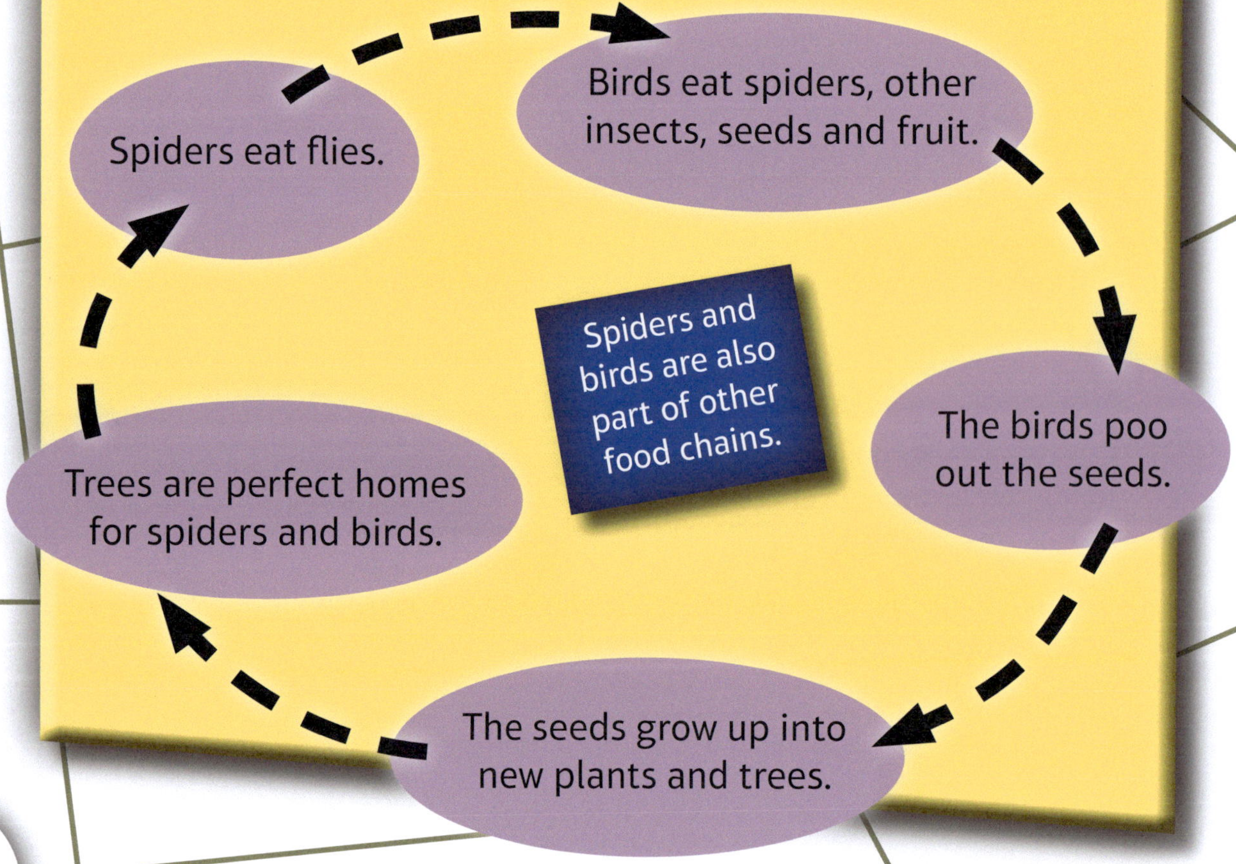

Spiders eat flies.

Birds eat spiders, other insects, seeds and fruit.

The birds poo out the seeds.

The seeds grow up into new plants and trees.

Trees are perfect homes for spiders and birds.

Spiders and birds are also part of other food chains.

28 **Set Up an Insect Retreat**
Pile up some logs and sticks together outside so that insects can live there.

29 **Plant a Tree**
Plant a tree in your backyard and watch it grow.

30 **Clean Up!**
Get your friends together and clean up an area near your home or school.

31 **Build a Bird a Home**
Ask a grown-up to help you make a birdhouse for the local birds.

32 **Don't Drop It**
Protect the native animals near your home by putting rubbish in the bin. Animals can get caught in, or hurt themselves on, rubbish left on the ground.

33 **Watch It!**
Look outside and try to spot some animals. Are they using your insect retreat or birdhouse? See ideas 28 and 31.

FAST FACT
Trees remove greenhouse gases from the air and make oxygen for us to breathe.

WEAR LESS

No, this doesn't mean you have to walk around in your undies to save Earth! It really means "have fewer clothes in your wardrobe". But hang on – how can that help?

How do clothes affect the world?

Everyone has a cotton T-shirt in their wardrobe. But have you ever thought about what happens before that T-shirt ends up with you?

Growing cotton

Chemicals are usually used to grow the cotton. These chemicals are bad for the environment.

↓

T-shirts travel a long way ...

The cotton has to go from the field to the cotton mill and then to the factory to be made into a T-shirt.

↓

And they travel even further ...

Many T-shirts are sold a long way from where they were made. What does this mean?

longer journeys = more greenhouse gases

So, why not just have a couple of T-shirts you love rather than lots? See? Wearing less clothing helps to save Earth!

FAST FACT

The chemicals used to grow and make cotton stay in the T-shirt fabric.

Top Tip!

See idea 37. Make sure you tell your mum or dad that you are swapping some clothes with a friend!

35 **Stop Growing?**
As you grow, your clothes will get too small. Don't throw them out – why not give them to charity?

36 **Look at the Label**
Before you buy clothes, have a look at the label inside. Try to buy clothes that are made closer to home.

37 **Run a Swapshop**
Bored with your clothes? Swap them with friends!

38 **Check Out Charity**
You don't always have to buy new clothes. See what clothes you can find in a second-hand shop.

39 **Wash Less**
Not you – your clothes! Some clothes don't need to be washed after every wear. Socks and undies probably do though!

40 **Glasses Giveaway**
Give your old glasses to a charity.

MAKE YOUR GRANNY HAPPY

Make your granny happy *and* save the world? Sounds impossible, but it's easy! On cold days, all you need to do is wear that jumper she knitted you for your birthday!

How can jumpers save Earth?

If your granny doesn't knit, don't worry. You can save the world with any jumper. Once you've put that jumper on, you'll realise how warm it is. Now, persuade everyone else in your house to put a jumper on, too. Are you all getting really warm? Better turn off your heating.

Why turn off the heating?

Well, the heating in most buildings is powered by electricity. Electricity is usually made from burning fossil fuels such as coal. Gas is a fossil fuel, too.

So every time you turn off the heating, you will help save the planet just a little bit.

Electricity or gas used for heating

Fossil fuels burnt

Greenhouse gases released

Global warming

Top Tip!

Turning the heating off, or down, can be difficult. Ask a grown-up to help you!

FAST FACT

About 11% of an average household's greenhouse gas **emissions** come from heating and cooling the house.

42 **Put On a Hat**

We lose lots of heat through our heads. Putting on a hat is an easy way to stay warm.

43 **Toasty Toes**

Wear extra-thick socks to keep your toes happy.

44 **Keep Warm at Night**

Take a hot water bottle to bed. If you don't have one, use an extra blanket instead.

45 **Ban the Draft**

Shut doors and windows to keep the heat in.

46 **On the Spot**

Feeling cold? Try running on the spot. How do you feel now?

47 **Hug Your Friend!**

Hug a friend or pet and you'll soon feel warm.

DON'T BE A STANDBY SUCKER

Who'd have thought you could save the world by flicking a switch? The switch is … the off switch! That's the *proper* off switch, not the "standby".

What's wrong with standby?

Lots of people turn things off by using the standby button. But "standby" is not really "off" because it still uses a tiny bit of electricity. Most of this electricity is made by burning fossil fuels. This produces greenhouse gases, which add to global warming. When you turn things off *properly*, they stop using electricity.

less electricity used = less greenhouse gases

Congratulations! With the flick of a switch you've helped save Earth!

Top Tip!
Check with a grown-up before turning things off. Not everything can be turned off. Fridges have to stay on all the time!

Poster Power

Design a poster to remind people to turn things off.

Start a "No TV Day"

For one day, switch the TV off and do something else instead.

Turn Off the Lights

But make sure there's no one else in the room first!

Think Fast

Hungry? Don't stare into the fridge with the door open. Decide what you want and close it fast.

Be Bright

Use energy-saving light globes. They use less energy than other globes.

Summer Sun

Dry your hair naturally when the weather is warm instead of using a hairdryer.

Want ideas for your "no TV day"? See ideas 63 to 69.

55 WASTE NOT, WANT NOT

"Waste not, want not" means don't throw things away carelessly. "Wasting not" is also a good way to help save Earth from being buried under a mountain of rubbish.

What do we waste?

Every year, we throw away tonnes and tonnes of rubbish. In one year, Australians throw away about:

- 80 million plastic bags
- $5 billion worth of food
- 500 million disposable coffee cups.

Here are three things you can do to stop the rubbish piling up.

Reduce

Reduce the amount of waste you produce. Try to choose things that have little or no wrapping.

Reuse

Try to reuse things instead of throwing them away.

Recycle

If you do have to throw things away, check to see if they can go in a recycling bin.

Blow Your Nose
When you get a cold or a sniffle, use a handkerchief and not a tissue!

Read Your Rubbish
Learn the recycling symbols and make sure you're recycling as much as you can.

Carry On Shopping
The next time you go shopping, use a cloth bag or an old plastic bag.

One In, One Out
Make someone's day. When you get a new toy, give an old one away!

Take Care
If you look after your things properly, they will last longer. Then, you won't need to keep buying replacements.

Buy Second-Hand Stuff
It helps reduce waste, and means fewer new things need to be made.

Learn to Fix Things
Try fixing something that's broken instead of replacing it.

Each year, the average Australian household creates 1.3 tonnes of landfill waste.

Want more hints for reusing things? Go to ideas 79 to 83.

63 MAKE A MONSTROUS SOCK

A lot of what we throw away is stuff that could be reused and made into something fun!

How can sock monsters save the world?

They can't do it by themselves – they're not superheroes! But with your help, they can put your old socks to good use.

You will need:

- 1 old sock
- stuffing (old fabric cut up)
- scissors, needle and thread
- 2 buttons.

1. Turn your sock inside out with the heel facing up.

2. Cut down the middle of the toe to make two ears. Sew along the edge of the ears to close them.

3. Turn your sock the right way out, stuff it with the old fabric then sew up the bottom.

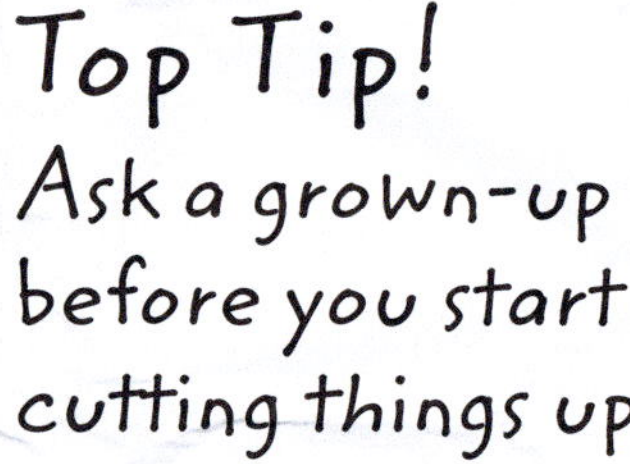

Top Tip!
Ask a grown-up before you start cutting things up.

64 Brilliant Birthday Cards

Fold a piece of card in half and cover it with pictures from magazines. Then, write your own message inside.

65 Sleepy Shopping Bag

Sew some handles on an old pillowcase to make a bag. Decorate it with old buttons or fabric.

66 Old Is New

Instead of throwing out old clothes you can alter them so they look new.

67 Reuse Your Old Jeans

Use the leg of old jeans as a door draught stopper. Cut off a jean leg, stuff it with old fabric or plastic bags, and sew up both ends.

68 Jar Holders

Jars can hold pens, coins and much more.

69 Think Outside the Box

Why don't you look at your rubbish and think of new ways to reuse it?

4. Sew on the two buttons to make eyes.

5. Push in the heel to make a mouth. Sew it in place, so it doesn't pop out. Your sock monster is finished!

70 SEE THE WORLD BY BIKE!

Every time you use the car, you add to global warming. That's because car engines release a greenhouse gas called carbon dioxide. So, another way to save Earth is to stop being driven around in cars!

Top Tip!
Remember to wear a helmet and make sure someone knows where you are going.

Bring on the bike

Bikes are *much* better than cars, for lots of reasons. The main one is that they don't release greenhouse gases. Oh, and they don't get stuck in traffic jams either!

A bike can take you practically everywhere. The next time you plan to go somewhere, think "Can I go by bike?"

FAST FACT
Many trips in cars are short enough to cycle instead. For example, the average trip in Melbourne is 2.9 kilometres.

71

Use Human Power

If you don't have a bike, how about skateboarding, walking or rollerblading?

72

Hop On the Train or Bus

If it's raining, go by public transport. Trains and buses burn less fossil fuel per passenger than cars.

73

The Walking Group

Ask to start a walking group to and from school if you can't ride your bike.

74

Give Someone a Lift

If you and your friend are going to the same place, give them a lift. That means only one car makes the trip, not two cars.

75

Wind Up the Windows

If you *do* travel by car, try not to open the windows too much. Cars run better with the windows closed.

76

Go Slow

On long car journeys, ask the driver to travel at 90–105 kilometres per hour. Most cars use less fuel at this speed.

77

Plan a Day Out

The next time you plan a family trip, go somewhere you can get to by train, by bus or even on foot.

78 LOVE A LIBRARY

Help save the world by reading books! As long as they're not brand-new books, that is. Instead, borrow them from a library. That way fewer new books need to be printed!

Recycling paper is good ...

A lot of the recycling from people's homes is paper. It comes from books, newspapers, magazines and **packaging**. The paper is taken away and recycled into new paper. Recycled paper is much better for the planet than non-recycled paper – fewer trees are cut down.

But using less paper is better

Even recycled paper harms the planet. Making it still produces **pollution** and adds to global warming. So, whenever possible, try to use less paper.

You can use old paper in your worm composter. See idea 11.

79 **Double It**
Print, or write, on both sides of a sheet of paper.

80 **Start a Book Group**
Swap books with your friends, especially this one!

81 **Resend It**
Reuse envelopes. All you need to do is open the envelope carefully, cover the address with a plain white sticker and you're good to go.

82 **Perfect Pad**
Make your own scrap-paper pad. Use it for notes and messages.

83 **Reuse Newspapers**
Make your own paper plates. Cut up old newspapers and soak them in water. Then, press onto a plate and wait for it to dry. Easy!

84 **New Ideas**
While you're taking the bus to the library (see idea 72), think of some other paper-related ways to reduce, reuse or recycle paper.

85 **No More Mail**
Stop unwanted junk mail. Make a "no junk mail" sign for your letter box.

86 GET TOILET TRAINED

Want to know one of the world's biggest problems right now? It's a lack of water. All around the world, countries are running out of water.

Why is it happening?

- Humans use more water in their homes than they did in the past.
- The world's population is increasing, but the amount of fresh water stays the same. This means there is less water for each person.
- More water is being used in farming and industry than in the past.

How can we change things?

Using less water is extremely important – humans, animals and plants cannot live without water.

One way to save water is to not flush the toilet so much.

After doing a wee, don't flush! But, make sure you close the toilet lid. If people don't like the idea, explain that wee is harmless. But, make sure you flush that other stuff down – poo. Yuck! It is very unhealthy to leave it lying around.

FAST FACT

Every time you flush the toilet, it uses up to 12 litres of water. That's six times as much as a person needs to drink each day! So, use the half flush whenever you can. It uses much less water than the full flush.

Top Tip!
Not everyone will like you leaving a wee in their toilet, so only do it if you think they won't mind. It's probably best not to do this at school!

If it's yellow, let it mellow.

If it's brown, flush it down.

Ban Drips!

Dripping taps can waste up to 90 litres of water a week!

Slow the Flow

Install a water-saving showerhead. These are one of the best ways to cut down your water use.

Shower Power

Make sure your showers are 3 minutes or under. Each minute you cut from your shower saves between 9 to 22 litres of water.

Please Your Parents!

Offer to do the washing up. Don't rinse the dishes with running water. Fill a separate bowl with clean water to rinse in.

Teeth Time

Only turn on the tap to rinse your toothbrush and your mouth. You can also use a glass of water to rinse your mouth.

92 BE A ROLE MODEL

Many adults come from a time when no one really bothered much about saving Earth. This is not their fault – hardly anyone knew back then that Earth *needed* saving!

Spread the word

You are now armed with lots of ideas to help save Earth. Make sure you share what you know with all your friends and family. After all, lots of people acting in the same way can make things a *lot* better.

Why not start with your school? Think about the things you would like to do differently. Speak to your classmates and teachers. Are you ready to spread the word and make a difference?

FAST FACT

When **Earth Day** was first celebrated on 22 April 1970, just one country took part. In 2010, 175 countries celebrated the day.

Top Tip!

Remember to ask before changing anything at school.

SAVE THE EARTH TODAY

I would like:

- more places to put bikes
- monthly swapshops for clothes and toys
- recycling bins in every classroom
- walking groups
- a "Get to school without a car" day

Hold a Waste Test

Ask if you can check the school's bins before they're collected. Can you think of ways to reduce the amount of rubbish?

Celebrate!

Why not get your school to celebrate Earth Day?

Get Sponsored

Do a sponsored walk, swim or cycle to raise money for an environmental charity.

Be a Green Author

Make a "green" book, like this one, explaining to other children what they can do to help save Earth.

97

Change a Friend

No, don't swap them! Just persuade one friend to do an activity from this book.

Look Back

Go back through the book. Which activities can you do at school?

Green Days

Start a "green" diary. Record all the things you do to help save the world.

100 THINK DIFFERENTLY

Things only change when someone wonders why things are the way they are – and whether they could be better. Great news – you've already started to think differently by reading this book!

Things only change when someone wonders ...

101 **Ask It!**
What question will you ask today?

why things are the way they are.

GLOSSARY

atmosphere layer of gases surrounding a planet

Earth Day a day chosen each year for people to think about looking after Earth

emissions something sent out or discharged

fertiliser substance which makes plants grow better

food chain series of plants and animals in which each one serves as food for the next in the chain

fossil fuels energy resources formed from the remains of plants and animals from millions of years ago (which will eventually run out)

free-range living in open spaces, not cages

global warming increase in the temperature of Earth, affecting weather patterns and environments

greenhouse gases gases that cause global warming

nutritional healthy, nourishing

packaging wrapping that goes around things we buy

pollution materials that cause harm to the natural world

INDEX